Beastly
BODY
EXPERIMENTS

Nick Arnold

Illustrated by **Dave Smith**

Visit Nick Arnold at

Scholastic Children's Books,
Euston House, 24 Eversholt Street,
London, NW1 1DB, UK

A division of Scholastic Ltd
London ~ New York ~ Toronto ~ Sydney ~ Auckland
Mexico City ~ New Delhi ~ Hong Kong

First published in the UK by Scholastic Ltd, 2008
Text copyright © Nick Arnold, 2008
Illustrations by Dave Smith, based on the style of the original
Horrible Science artwork by Tony De Saulles
Illustrations © Dave Smith 2008
All rights reserved

ISBN 978 1407 10359 4

Printed and bound by Tien Wah Press Pte. Ltd, Malaysia

2 4 6 8 10 9 7 5 3 1

The right of Nick Arnold and Dave Smith to be identified as the author and
illustrator of this work respectively has been asserted by them in accordance with the Copyright,
Designs and Patents Act, 1988.

CONTENTS

INTRODUCTION

Mention blood and guts to most people and they'll shudder and say

UGH— HOW BEASTLY!

And you can see why! I mean, this book is bursting with stomach-turning squishy blood and guts – but I bet that won't put you off. After all, you're still reading, and you look as if you're itching to try a few beastly experiments and train as a Horrible Scientist too! Of course this is not a job for the faint-hearted and might freak out your family and revolt your relatives – but they'll have to put up with it because it's all in the cause of Science!

So read on, brave reader. You'll be training under the guidance of our very own Horrible Science expert Dr Grimgrave. The doc knows his medicine, but be warned – he's not exactly a laugh a minute. In fact, he hasn't even smiled since 1962...

I DON'T FIND THIS INTRODUCTION THE LEAST BIT AMUSING.

IT TICKLED MY FUNNY BONE.

DR GRIMGRAVE – THE WORLD'S MOST DISMAL DOCTOR.

DR G'S SKELETON.

After a hard day being rude to patients (and even curing a few of them) Dr Grimgrave likes to unwind with a few grisly body experiments. Let's go and join him...

TEST YOUR BODY

Before you're allowed to get to grips with beastly body bits, Dr Grimgrave wants to give you A VERY SERIOUS WARNING. I told you he was a dismal doc!

DR GRIMGRAVE'S RULES FOR EXPERIMENTS

1 Always read the experiment before starting it. (Only idiots ignore their doctor's orders.)

2 Make sure you have the necessary equipment before you start. Here are some items that you'll be using rather a lot.

YOU'D BETTER READ THESE RULES FIRST – OR ELSE...

OR ELSE HE'LL READ THE RIOT ACT...

NOTEBOOK AND PENCIL

ADULT ASSISTANT

TAPE MEASURE

MEASURING JUG

3 Always obey the warning signs. Anyone who ignores these vital safety precautions will be dosed with extra-strong anti-constipation medicine.

HORRIBLE DANGER WARNING!
Order your adult assistant to do any dangerous task. If they get burnt, cut or scalded make sure they go straight to hospital and don't pester their long-suffering doctor!

HORRIBLE MESS WARNING!
Put down newspaper and wear old clothes for these experiments (and remember that blood does tend to ruin carpets!).

HORRIBLE DIFFICULTY WARNING!
Order your adult assistant to attempt the annoyingly tricky bits and blame them if they ruin your experiment.

4 Always clear up after your experiments. Anyone who ignores this rule will be put to work scrubbing out my mouldy medical specimen jars.

YOU HAVE BEEN WARNED!!

PONG

WHIFF

OR IT'S THE NASTY MEDICINE FOR YOU!

Before we're allowed to start the first experiment, Dr Grimgrave is insisting that we learn these science words off by heart...

DR. GRIMGRAVE'S
DREADFUL
DICTIONARY

Words every patient needs to know in order not to pester their hardworking, long-suffering doctor with idiotic questions.

 CELL – microscopic blob of living matter. Your body is made up of billions of these.

 GENE – a chemical code found inside most cells. Your genes order your cells to grow and build a complete, fully functioning human body. Just make sure YOU look after it for the rest of your life!

ATOM – a ball of matter millions of times smaller than a cell.

MOLECULE – a group of two or more atoms joined together.

PROTEIN – a type of complex molecule that forms many body substances.

ATOMS ARE EVEN SMALLER THAN MY PATIENTS' BRAINS, HA HA!

THE INSIDE-OUT BODY

MANY OF MY IDIOT PATIENTS HAVE NO IDEA WHAT'S INSIDE THEIR BODIES. I USE THIS EXPERIMENT TO SHOW THEM...

AND THEY SOON REGRET ASKING!

WHAT YOU NEED:
- **White swing-bin liner with tie handles** • **Scissors**
- **Water-based felt pens (black, brown, green, yellow and red for a nice ruddy bloody colour)** • **This book**
- **Red tee-shirt (not too vital)** • **Tape measure**
- **Damp cloth to wipe away embarrassing errors**

WHAT YOU DO:

1 When you pull the swing-bin liner off the roll it looks like this. Use the tape measure to measure from the bottom of your neck to 5 cm below your hips. Next measure the same distance on the swing-bin liner and mark it with the pen.

2 Use the scissors to cut off the bottom edge of the swing-bin liner below your mark.

3 Study the picture below…

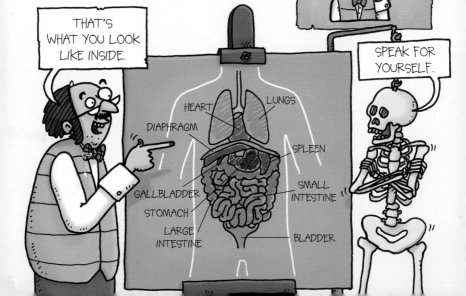

THAT'S WHAT YOU LOOK LIKE INSIDE.

SPEAK FOR YOURSELF.

HEART

LUNGS

DIAPHRAGM

SPLEEN

GALLBLADDER

SMALL INTESTINE

STOMACH

LARGE INTESTINE

BLADDER.

4 Your mission (if you're brave enough) is to copy this on to one side of the bag. To do this you need to open the bag up and lay it flat on a table. It's best to outline the body bits in black and wipe away any mistakes with the damp cloth.

5 When your body bits are drawn you can colour them in with felt pens. Wait for the ink to dry.

6 It helps if you wear a red or pink tee-shirt. Carefully put on the body overall with your arms through the tie holes. Admire yourself in the mirror before making your grand entrance and flabbergasting your family…

WHAT HAPPENS:
The picture of the insides fits perfectly over your own body and matches where your real body bits are hidden under your skin.

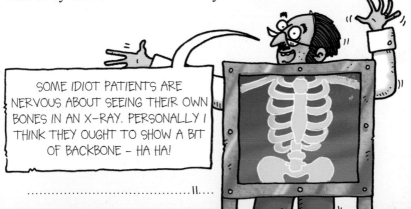

SOME IDIOT PATIENTS ARE NERVOUS ABOUT SEEING THEIR OWN BONES IN AN X-RAY. PERSONALLY I THINK THEY OUGHT TO SHOW A BIT OF BACKBONE - HA HA!

THIS IS BECAUSE:

All human bodies have the same body bits and hopefully you're not missing any vital bits and pieces…

Bet you never knew!

In many parts of the world people once ate other human beings – it's called "cannibalism". Oh, so you knew that? Well, I bet you never knew any cannibal recipes. An 1870s' recipe from the New Hebrides Islands in the Pacific involved breaking all the bones in the body, cutting off the head, pulling out the guts and filling the body with some nice healthy fruit and veg. The body was baked in a pit of hot stones and the cannibals took the grisly leftovers home to their families. Mind you, if they were vegetarian cannibals I expect they ate Swedes…

A VERY POLITE NOTE FROM THE PUBLISHERS

WE WOULD LIKE TO WARN READERS WHO ARE FEELING HUNGRY THAT WE DON'T ENCOURAGE CANNIBALISM.
IN FACT IT'S AGAINST THE LAW TO EAT:
A) FRIENDS AND FAMILY (INCLUDING LITTLE BROTHERS)
B) ADULT ASSISTANTS (YOU'LL BE NEEDING THEIR HELP LATER IN THIS BOOK)
C) TEACHERS (EXCEPT IN AN EMERGENCY).
AND SAYING "I FELT A BIT PECKISH" ISN'T A GOOD ENOUGH EXCUSE!

SOMETHING'S A-FOOT

HUMANS' BODIES ARE USUALLY IN PROPORTION. THAT'S WHY PEOPLE WITH BIG HEADS GENERALLY HAVE LARGER BODIES...

CERTAIN DOCTORS ARE MORE BIG-HEADED THAN THE REST OF US...

WHAT YOU NEED:
- A tape measure • Notebook and pencil
- A good friend (in an emergency you could pretend that your adult assistant is a good friend)

WHAT YOU DO:
1 Measure the distance between the crease in the crook of your friend's elbow to the crease where their wrist joins their hand. Write these figures down.

2 Measure the length of their foot (they will need to take their shoes off and you will need to hold your breath if their feet are smelly). Write down this figure if you're still conscious. OK – you can breathe now!

3 Ask your friend to stand with their arms spread wide. Measure the distance from the tip of their longest finger to the tip of the longest finger on their other hand. You

might need your adult assistant to lend a hand (or even two hands) for this job. Write down this measurement.

4 Finally, measure your friend's height and write it down.

WHAT HAPPENS:

Your figures for steps 1 and 2 should be the same or close. And so should your figures for steps 3 and 4.

THIS IS BECAUSE:

The size of your body is controlled by your genes (see page 8). Your genes ensure that your body grows in proportion and you don't end up with one hand much bigger than the other or something.

Bet you never knew!

It's possible to have a hand that doesn't belong to you. In 1998 French surgeons sewed a dead man's hand on to a New Zealand man. The New Zealander had lost his own hand in an accident – but three years later he had the hand removed. He didn't want it. These days hand transplants are performed in many countries – I guess surgeons like to lend a hand, ha ha.

ON LOAN

TAKE A BREATHER!

Are you still breathing? Well, hopefully you are!

IF YOU'RE NOT BREATHING SEEK MEDICAL AID IMMEDIATELY!

OTHERWISE YOU'LL END UP LIKE ME!

In this breathtakingly exhausting experiment you'll find out how much air you puff out and why breathing is something you can't put off until next week…

WHAT YOU NEED:

- **Watch with a second hand**
- **Your trusty tape measure**
- **Measuring jug**
- **Waterproof felt pen**
- **Funnel**
- **Notebook and pen**
- **2-litre plastic bottle of your favourite drink (don't forget to slurp up the drink first!)**
- **A clean rubber or plastic tube at least 30 cm long. Ideally this should be as wide as can fit into the neck of the bottle. If you don't have a tube you could use a large balloon**
- **Your good friend from the previous experiment**

I'M DEAD THIRSTY!

WHAT YOU DO:

AAHHHH

1 Take a few deep breaths. Then take the deepest breath you can and sing an Ahhhhhhhhhhhhh! note for as long as you can (don't do this at 5 am or your parents might do something that will make you shout AGGGGGGGGGGGH! instead). Don't stop until you've run out of puff. Ask your good friend to time you and note down this figure.

2 Ask your friend to measure the distance around your chest and note this figure too.

3 Take a few more deep breaths and ask your friend to measure the distance around your chest when your lungs are full of air. Once again they should note down the figure.

4 Next fill the measuring jug with 100 ml of water and use the funnel to pour it into the bottle. Mark the water level with your pen. Repeat this step until the bottle is full of water.

5 You need to do the next part of the experiment in the kitchen sink or the bath. Fill your bath or sink and lay the bottle in the water. Make sure the bottle contains as little air as possible.

IN MY VIEW ALL CHILDREN SHOULD TAKE THEIR BATHS IN COLD WATER. IT SAVES ON THE HEATING BILLS, YOU KNOW.

I'D CATCH MY DEATH OF COLD.

SPLOSH

RATTL

6 Place the tube in the mouth of the bottle. Hold the bottle upright and upside down whilst keeping its mouth underwater. Take a few deep breaths and then blow through the tube for as hard and long as you can.

7 If you're using the balloon, blow it up and let the air out of it a few times until it's saggy. Take a few deep breaths and blow as much air as you can into the balloon. Hold the balloon neck tightly so that the air can't escape. As in step 6, you'll need to hold the bottle upside down with its mouth underwater. Next, push the neck of the balloon into the bottle and slowly let the air out. Once again, you need to ensure the mouth of the bottle stays underwater.

8 Explain to your family that the bubbles they can hear in the bath are nothing to do with the beans you had for supper.

WHAT HAPPENS:

The air pushes the water out of the bottle and the 100 ml marks will show you how much air you breathe out. You may find that your lungs can hold more than two litres of air. If the bottle empties, you can hold your breath and quickly refill it with water. You can then continue the experiment with the rest of your breath.

THIS IS BECAUSE:

HE'S HOLDING MY BREATH...

Steps 1 and 2 are simple ways to measure how much air your lungs can hold. Steps 4 to 7 provide a more exact method.

Bet you never knew!

1 You breathe 23,000 times a day. (If you don't believe me you can always count your breaths – just don't do it too loudly in the middle of the night.)

2 There's an interestingly horrible lung disease in which water sloshes in the chest around the lungs. This causes odd noises when the patient breathes and a loud SPLOSH! when they jump up and down.

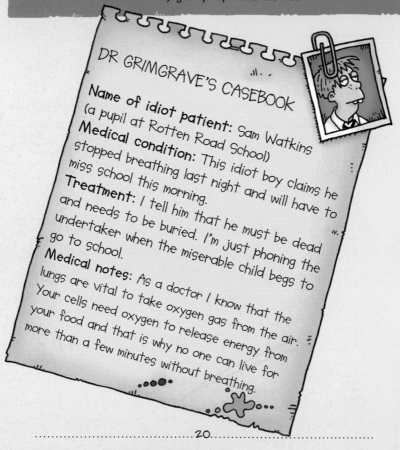

DR GRIMGRAVE'S CASEBOOK

Name of idiot patient: Sam Watkins (a pupil at Rotten Road School)

Medical condition: This idiot boy claims he stopped breathing last night and will have to miss school this morning.

Treatment: I tell him that he must be dead and needs to be buried. I'm just phoning the undertaker when the miserable child begs to go to school.

Medical notes: As a doctor I know that the lungs are vital to take oxygen gas from the air. Your cells need oxygen to release energy from your food and that is why no one can live for more than a few minutes without breathing.

WHAT A YAWN!

> I HATE YAWNING. MY IDIOT PATIENTS YAWN IN MY FACE WHEN I DESCRIBE PERFECTLY SIMPLE SCIENTIFIC PRINCIPLES. THEY NEED TO TAKE A COLD SHOWER FIRST THING IN THE MORNING – IT WORKS FOR ME!

WHAT YOU NEED:
• **Yourself** • **A group of people** • **A large warm room (a classroom will do just fine)**

WHAT YOU DO:
Pretend to yawn. DON'T overdo it otherwise your teacher will get suspicious. Your job is to fool people that you *really* are yawning.

TERRIBLE TIP
You may like to practise yawning in private to rehearse your Oscar-winning performance!

WHAT HAPPENS:

One or two people will yawn. With luck you'll start the whole class yawning their heads off – including your teacher!

THIS IS BECAUSE:

In 2007 US scientists suggested people yawn in order to cool their brains and stay alert. We may even yawn together as a signal designed to keep us on the ball. So yawning in class isn't bad manners – tell that to your teacher!

SOUNDS A YAWN TO ME.

Bet you never knew!

So you knew that cats yawn? And dogs too? Well, I bet you never knew that birds and fishes yawn too...

HAIRY MOMENTS

Dr Grimgrave has refused to take part in this experiment on the grounds that he hasn't got any hair to experiment with…

BALDNESS IS NO LAUGING MATTER!

KEEP YOUR HAIR ON, DR G!

WHAT YOU NEED:

- One hair – the longer the better. It could be yours or from a good friend but there's no need to pluck the cat!
- 3 pencils • A small box (I used an empty matchbox drawer 12 cm x 7 cm) • Scissors and parcel tape
- Heavy object such as a chopping board or a boring medical textbook (as read by Dr Grimgrave)
- Kitchen scales • Some coins

EVIL IDEA

Hmmm…

Ask your adult assistant for the coins and absent-mindedly spend them before the adult asks for them back.

WHAT YOU DO:

1 Pull open one end of the box to make a flap…

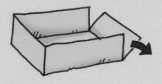

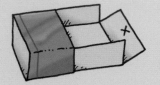

2 Wrap the parcel tape around the end like so…

3 Carefully place one end of your hair at point "X". Stick a piece of parcel tape over this end of the hair and wrap the ends of the parcel tape around the cardboard flap. Press the tape down and make sure it's sticking firmly to the hair.

TERRIBLE TIP
It helps if you hold the hair against a bright light so you can see it easily.

4 Wrap the other end of the hair around a pencil. And stick another piece of parcel tape around the hair.

5 Set up the two other pencils like this…

6 Next place the pencil with your hair and box attached to it on top of the two pencils…

7 Now for the interesting bit! Carefully place your coins one by one in the bottom of the box. Continue doing this until the hair breaks.

8 Weigh the box and the coins.

WHAT HAPPENS:

It's amazing how strong your hair is! My hair held up the box and 50 g of coins – hundreds of times its own weight. Is your hair any tougher than that?

THIS IS BECAUSE:

Oh, it looks like Dr G is back now we're talking about science...

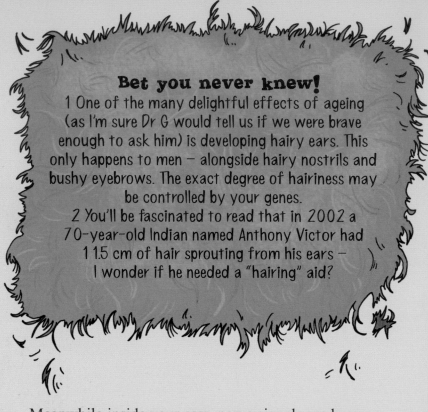

Bet you never knew!

1 One of the many delightful effects of ageing (as I'm sure Dr G would tell us if we were brave enough to ask him) is developing hairy ears. This only happens to men — alongside hairy nostrils and bushy eyebrows. The exact degree of hairiness may be controlled by your genes.

2 You'll be fascinated to read that in 2002 a 70-year-old Indian named Anthony Victor had 11.5 cm of hair sprouting from his ears — I wonder if he needed a "hairing" aid?

Meanwhile inside your ears, nerve signals are busy buzzing your brain. D'you fancy giving your thinking gear a work-out?

BEASTLY BODY
Quiz

ALL THE ANSWERS TO THIS QUIZ ARE NUMBERS – YOU JUST HAVE TO MATCH THE FIGURES TO THE FACTS...

I'LL JUST HAVE TO FIGURE IT OUT!

FACTS

1. If you didn't have any blood, you'd be _____ per cent lighter.
2. _____ is a typical pulse rate per minute for an elderly person. (Don't test Granny to prove it.)
3. Phosphorus is a poisonous chemical that glows in the dark. Your body is _____ per cent phosphorus.
4. If your teacher had a body without any bones, she'd be _____ per cent lighter.

NUMBERS TO CHOOSE

a) 60
b) 14
c) 8
d) 1

I'VE GOT BONES WITHOUT ANY BODY.

Answers:

1 c) You'd also be 101 per cent dead.

2 a) It was about 130 when you were born and slowed over time.

3 d) Fortunately it's found in all your bones. If all your phosphorus was in one place your funny bone might glow in the dark...

4 b) Amazingly your bones contain over 20 per cent water, but this doesn't explain why your bones turn to water when you have to take a science test.

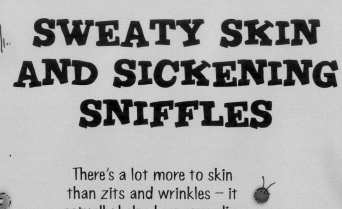

SWEATY SKIN AND SICKENING SNIFFLES

There's a lot more to skin
than zits and wrinkles – it
actually helps keep you alive
by shielding you from germs.
In fact you could say that the
Horrible Science of skin is a lot
more than er, skin deep...

ARE YOU A DRIP?

SKIN KEEPS YOUR BODY COOL BY PERSPIRING – OR SWEATING AS VULGAR PEOPLE CALL IT. I HATE IDIOT PATIENTS DRIPPING IN MY WAITING ROOM AND THEIR DAMP HANDSHAKES ARE SO UNHYGIENIC!

DON'T LOOK AT ME – I'M BONE DRY...

HACK

WHAT YOU NEED:
- A polythene bag (a large freezer bag is ideal)
- An elastic band • A hand (you should find one attached to your wrist)
- A watch

WHAT YOU DO:
1 Make sure your hand is really dry (not like Dr G's patients). Place your hand inside the bag (and I mean your hand and not your HEAD – don't forget the Horrible Danger Warning on page 10!)

TERRIBLE TIP
It helps if the hand is not the one you write with (for example right-handed people should place the bag over their left hand).

2 Wrap the elastic band around your wrist to secure the bag.

3 Leave the bag over your hand for 15 minutes to see what happens…

WHAT HAPPENS:

Your hand starts to feel clammy and the sides of the bag start to fog up.

AND DON'T WRAP THE BAND TOO TIGHTLY – WE DON'T WANT ANY HANDS DROPPING OFF, HA HA! BUT IF THEY DO YOU COULD ALWAYS DONATE THEM TO MY PRIVATE MEDICAL COLLECTION...

THIS IS BECAUSE:

Your skin contains about two million sweat glands where sweat is made – there's about 370 in every square centimetre of your palms. The sweat escapes from tiny holes in our skin and some moisture escapes through your skin. The damp stuff evaporates (turns to water vapour – a gas formed from water molecules) and takes heat from your body into the air. In the experiment, the bag slowly fills with water vapour.

MOP

BAKE

SOME OF MY PATIENTS PERSPIRE MORE THAN OTHERS BUT THEY'RE A BIT WET, HA HA!

DR GRIMGRAVE'S CASEBOOK

Name of idiot patient: Harvey Tucker (Australian journalist)

Medical condition: Excessive heat. Mr Tucker emails me from California's Death Valley to say he's sweating and to ask if he is about to die. Death Valley is one of Earth's hottest places and temperatures above 42°C can kill a person.

Treatment: I advise him to shelter from the sun and drink plenty of water with a small amount of salt added to replace the sweat he's losing.

Medical notes: The idiot checked into a motel and spent the rest of the week living off fizzy drinks and ice cream.

GRRR – DISGRACEFUL! HE SHOULD HAVE BEEN EATING HEALTHY SALADS!

LOOKS LIKE DR G IS GETTING A BIT HEATED...

Bet you never knew!
Scientists will go to any lengths to solve a mystery and a group of brave scientists have even tested belly-button fluff. They found out it was made of dried sweat and fibres from your clothes. So now you know!

SICKENING SNIFFLES

* ENGLISH TRANSLATION: THE COLD IS WIDESPREAD. IT'S CAUSED BY TINY MICROBES MANY TIMES SMALLER THAN BACTERIA.

WHAT YOU NEED:

- A clean empty plant spray
- 80-cm length of clingfilm
- Blu-Tack
- Notebook and pencil
- Tape measure
- Torch

HORRIBLE DANGER WARNING!

Check with your adult assistant to make sure the container is clean and not full of weedkiller. You can always offer them a vomit bag if they get poisoned.

WHAT YOU DO:

1 Wash out the spray container with plenty of clean water a few times and then fill the container with water.

2 Fix the clingfilm by its corners to a low beam or doorway so it hangs free. Younger readers should order their adult assistant to do this job and fall off their chair. Make sure you can clearly see the torch through the clingfilm. The torch should be at least a metre behind the clingfilm.

3 Whilst your adult assistant is receiving treatment for their injuries, measure 1.5 metres from the clingfilm. Fire the spray at the clingfilm.

WHAT HAPPENS:

The clingfilm sways slightly as if in a breeze. Look carefully and you'll see that it's covered in tiny drops. They show up better when you switch the light on.

THIS IS BECAUSE:
CONGRATULATIONS!
You've made an artificial sneeze! Before you sneeze, you breathe in sharply. Then your airways close and you squeeze the air in your chest and suddenly let it out – all without thinking! A sneeze can contain up to 5,000 snotty, germ-laden droplets that fly 4 metres and spatter anyone within range.

SNEEZING IS CAUSED BY COLDS, DUST OR IRRITATING SUBSTANCES. MY IDIOT PATIENTS OFTEN FORGET TO USE A HANDKERCHIEF AND BLAST GERMS IN MY FACE. FORTUNATELY I'M IMMUNE* TO THE GERMS

*IMMUNE = DR G'S WHITE BLOOD CELLS CAN RECOGNIZE AND DESTROY THE GERMS.

DR GRIMGRAVE'S CASEBOOK
Name of idiot patient:
Sam Watkins (NOT my favourite patient!)
Medical condition: This annoying boy can't stop sneezing. He claims he has a cold and can't go to school.
Treatment: Knowing the patient I become suspicious. Then I observe a pot of pepper in his pocket. Pepper contains irritating chemicals that cause sneezing. I order the boy to eat pepper on his cornflakes until he stops sneezing.

EDIBLE SNOT

SOME IDIOT PATIENTS HAVE BEEN OBSERVED TO INGEST THEIR OWN MUCUS.* DISGUSTING HABIT! I TEACH THEM A LESSON BY MAKING THEM TRY THIS EXPERIMENT...

IT'S SNOT VERY NICE...

PICK

WAGGLE

*ENGLISH TRANSLATION = EAT THEIR OWN SNOT

WHAT YOU NEED:

- **Measuring jug**
- **Kettle • Teaspoon**
- **Long-handled spoon for stirring**
- **Food colour (I use green for a revolting effect – or yellow for everyday snot) • Jelly (a yellowish jelly is best but red is OK in an emergency)**
- **Scissors • Adult assistant**
- **Golden syrup**

WHAT YOU DO:

1 Ask your adult to cut two small squares of jelly and put them in the measuring jug. Each square should be about 1.5 cm square – in all there should be 20–30 g of jelly.

2 Boil some water in the kettle.

3 Pour 100 ml of water over the jelly and stir well with your long-handled spoon until the jelly dissolves.

4 Whilst the adult's bandaging his wounds, add a drop of food colour to the mixture and stir.

HORRIBLE DANGER WARNING!
Younger readers should order their adult assistant into the danger zone for steps 2 and 3.

HORRIBLE MESS WARNING!
Take care – food colouring stains skin and clothes. You can take off your clothes – but removing your skin can prove a bit messy.

I FIND SCRUBBING WITH A HARD SCRATCHY PUMICE STONE DOES THE TRICK!

I OVERDID THE SKIN REMOVAL...

5 Add two teaspoonfuls of golden syrup to the mix and stir it until the syrup dissolves.

6 Place the jug and mixture in the fridge for eight hours or overnight.

WHAT HAPPENS:

The mixture has turned gloopy and looks horribly like thick snot. Of course you could try eating it but you ought to make sure it's not real...

ACTUALLY THAT'S A MEDICAL SAMPLE.

THIS IS BECAUSE:

Real snot is gloopy and stringy because it contains long stringy molecules of sugars and proteins. Water is trapped amongst the molecules, and the more water it contains the runnier your snot is. You may not like to read this, but your edible snot contains protein and sugar molecules too – and of course water. That's why it feels just like the real thing!

EVIL IDEA
Why not scoop a glob of edible snot in a hankie and pretend to sneeze it out in front of your little sister? Just don't scoff it in front of your family at mealtimes...

OR YOU'LL BE SENT TO BED WITHOUT ANY SUPPER!

Bet you never knew!
The slimy, gooey consistency of snot is ideal for trapping dust. Why not sprinkle a fine pepper on your edible snot to prove this? But DON'T EAT IT AFTERWARDS! Of course that's why snot is there – to trap dust and germs and help defend your body.

HOW TO MAKE YOUR OWN SHRUNKEN HEAD

The pride and joy of Dr Grimgrave's gruesome medical collection is this shrunken head from South America…

HERE'S HOW TO MAKE YOUR OWN SHRUNKEN HEAD WITHOUT DECAPITATING* ANYONE…

* POSH WORD FOR CUTTING SOMEONE'S HEAD OFF.

WHAT YOU NEED:
- An apple (try not to eat it before the experiment)
- 200 ml lemon juice • Vegetable peeler
- Apple corer • Tablespoon
- Salt • Tape measure • Notebook and pencil
- Plate or baking tray • Bowl • Table knife
- Raisins, wool and rice for decoration
- An oven and oven gloves

WHAT YOU DO:
1 Start off by measuring the circumference (distance around) your head – er, I mean apple. Write this figure in your notebook.

2 Remove the apple core with the corer and peel the apple with the peeler. (Younger readers should leave the boring coring and unappealing peeling to their adult assistant.)

3 Add the lemon juice to the bowl and mix in one tablespoon of salt. Roll the apple around in the salty juice until it's completely covered.

4 Set the oven on a cool setting (about 100°C). Younger readers should definitely order their adult assistant to do this.

HORRIBLE DANGER WARNING!

Cutting, ovens and heat = bloodshed and burns...

YOU HAVE BEEN WARNED!

TERRIBLE TIP

You need to make these features a little larger than life because the head will shrink (but of course!)

5 Use your knife to carve two eyes, a nose and a mouth for your shrunken head.

6 Place the head on the baking tray and put the tray in the oven. Leave it for about six hours until the apple has almost dried out.
7 Place raisins in the eyeholes and if you're feeling disgustingly creative you might like to add some strands of wool for hair and rice grains for the teeth.

WHAT HAPPENS:

The circumference of your shrunken head has shrunk by about 20 per cent. You can check this with your tape measure and note the figure in your notebook.

THIS IS BECAUSE:

Apples are made up of 80 per cent water. The salt helped to draw water from the apple. With less water inside it, the apple shrank. The brown colour is made when oxygen in the air combines with molecules in the apple to make new molecules.

EVIL IDEA
You're far too nice to scare your little sister with your revolting shrunken head...
AREN'T YOU?

What's that? You wanted a REAL shrunken head? Well, just for you – here's a method used by the Jivaro people of the Amazon Rainforest. It's sure to give you a head start...

How to shrink a human Head

1 You will need a human head.

2 Peel off the flesh and turn it inside out.

3 Feel free to put the skull on display to impress your friends.

4 Scrape the flesh clean of fat. Turn the head the right way out and sew up the mouth and eyeholes so its ghost can't escape and haunt you.

5 Simmer the head in a pot of water and wild berries for two hours. The flesh will shrink by about a third.

6 Heat some pebbles and place them inside the head to shrink the flesh some more.

7 Carry on heating the head between two fires and fill it with hot sand until it shrinks to the exact size you want. By now your head will be black.

8 Rub your head with berries and charcoal to stop the skin from cracking. Don't forget to give it a scary haircut.

9 Hang it from your neck for a special celebration.

I USED TO BE A HEAD TEACHER.

I CAN SEE YOU'RE NO BONEHEAD...

GRUESOME GOOSEBUMPS

WHAT YOU NEED:

- A good friend dressed in a tee-shirt
- A feather (if you don't have a feather, don't pluck the parrot – use a thin strip of tissue paper about 15 cm long and 3 cm wide)
- Teaspoon left in the fridge for two hours

WHAT YOU DO:

1 Sit your good friend down in a chair with their back to you.

2 Very gently stroke the back of their neck with the tip of the feather or tissue paper.

3 Wait five to ten minutes. Sit them down again if they happen to have moved. This time tell them they're about be tortured by having ice-cold water full of ice cubes trickled down the back of their neck.

HORRIBLE SCIENCE WARNING!
No, you don't actually use iced-water – that's too cruel even for Horrible Science!

4 V-e-r-y s-l-o-w-l-y and gently touch the back of their neck with the cold spoon…

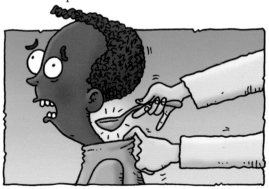

WHAT HAPPENS:

Your friend gets goosebumps at stage 2 and possibly stages 3 and 4.

THIS IS BECAUSE:

Your skin has about five million tiny hairs (there are about 100,000 larger hairs on your head ... unless you happen to be Dr G)...

WHEN YOU ARE COLD, TINY MUSCLES MAKE HAIRS STAND UP CAUSING SMALL BUMPS IN THE SKIN – GOOSEBUMPS. THIS REACTION IS ALSO CAUSED BY FEAR – AND I'LL GIVE YOU FEAR IF WE HAVE ANY MORE BALD REMARKS!

DR GRIMGRAVE'S CASEBOOK

Name of idiot patient:
Harvey Tucker (Not that idiot again!)

Medical condition: Goosebumps. This idiot patient emails me from the Arctic to say he has goosebumps. He wants to know if he will die of hypothermia. No such luck, unfortunately. Goosebumps are a normal result of cold or fear.

Treatment: I tell Mr Tucker to pull himself together and go for a brisk run to warm up.

Medical notes: Animals react in the same way. By fluffing up their fur they trap air against their skin and stay warm. It also makes them look bigger to warn off an attacker.

NASTY MEDICINE
QUIZ

DOCTORS IN THE PAST WERE EVEN BIGGER IDIOTS THAN MY PATIENTS. WHICH OF THESE SO-CALLED CURES DID THEY REALLY TRY AND WHICH IS A FORGERY?

2 To cure stupidity in children.
Tie the child to a length of wood and feed him powdered wood beetles. It's ideal for any child who is as thick as a plank!

1 To cure a headache.
Scrape the moss off a decaying skull and dry it into powder. Short the powder up your nose.

3 To cure fever in children.
Make them eat woodlice. If you can't find any woodlice they can munch mashed-up spiders and cobwebs instead.

4 If you get bitten by a mouse.
Roast and eat the mouse and put its skin and liver on the bite. If that doesn't work, try a powder made from the ground-up teeth of dead people.

ANSWERS:
1 True – USA 1833.
2 False – unless they happen to use it at your school.
3 True – it was a traditional 18th-century English remedy.
4 True – it was suggested by a Dr Stephen Brasnell in 1633.

And talking about teeth, the next chapter has plenty to get your dentures into...

THE GREEDY GOBBLING GUTS

Imagine you sat around all day eating and burping and gurgling and making other unmentionable noises. Well, there's one part of your beastly bod that does all that and worse. What am I talking about? Dr G knows!

THE ALIMENTARY CANAL* IS A FASCINATING PART OF THE BODY. I ENJOY WATCHING DOCUMENTARIES ABOUT IT WHILE I EAT MY SUPPER.

* MEDICAL TERM FOR THE GUTS

HAVE YOU GOT THE GUTS?

Sssh! Dr Grimgrave is with a patient…

NO, MR TUCKER YOU ARE NOT DYING. YOU FEEL SICK BECAUSE YOU'VE EATEN TOO MUCH ICE CREAM!

BUT I HAD A GUT FEELING ABOUT THIS…

Will your gut feeling allow you to try this disgusting digestive experiment?

WHAT YOU NEED:

- **An old pair of tights. Ask permission before raiding Granny's underwear drawer or you could find yourself in a tights spot…**
- **Scissors • Small bowl • A balloon (ideally poo coloured) • Large bowl of water (or potty if you want to be especially revolting)**
- **Olive oil • 30 cm of string**
- **Tape measure**

MY GRANNY WILL NEVER MISS THIS OLD PAIR OF TIGHTS…

• **A clip like this. If you haven't got one try using a large paperclip.**

WHAT YOU DO:

1 Fill the balloon with water until it's about 6 cm across and 15 cm long. Knot the end so that the water can't escape.

2 Knot one leg of the tights as close to the top of the leg as you can. (I hope your Granny wasn't wearing the tights when you did this.) You can then cut off the leg below the knot. (I *really* hope your Granny wasn't wearing the tights when you did this!)

3 Cut off the end of the remaining leg just where your Granny's toes would have been if she had been wearing the tights when you chopped her leg off.

4 Place the clip so it's pinching shut the top of the remaining leg.

5 Place the balloon in the bowl and pour the olive oil over it. Use your hands to make sure that the balloon is really slippery and slimy. Now for the beastly bit – place the slippery balloon in the waist of the tights and tie the string.

YOUR EXPERIMEN SHOULD LOC LIKE THIS.

6 Imagine the top of the tights is your stomach and the balloon is your breakfast. Your stomach squishes your cornflakes for about three hours but you only need do this for a few seconds.

7 Release the clip and squeeze the balloon along the leg of the tights.

WHAT HAPPENS:

You will find the easiest way to do this is to stretch the leg of the tights and pinch the fabric just BEHIND the balloon.

THIS IS BECAUSE:

The squeeze pushes the balloon forward.

BALLS OF FOOD ARE SQUEEZED FORWARD BY THE SIDES OF YOUR INTESTINES IN THE SAME WAY. WE DOCTORS CALL THIS PERISTALSIS.*

SQUEEZE

* THAT'S PER-RY-STAL-SIS.

EDIBLE POO

ULTIMATELY WASTE FOOD AND DEAD BACTERIA EMERGE IN THE FORM OF FAECES, OR "POO" AS IGNORANT PERSONS CALL IT...

AND THAT'S THE BOTTOM LINE.

WHAT YOU NEED:

- A bowl • Dessertspoon
- Tablespoon • Packet of chocolate sponge mix
- Tin of sweetcorn • Adult assistant
- Olive oil • Teaspoon

WHAT YOU DO:

1 Wash your hands before starting this experiment.

2 Add one heaped tablespoon of chocolate cake mix to the bowl and pour a tablespoonful of oil over the mix. Keep stirring until the mixture is a lovely revolting brown goo.

I WANT TO SEE THOSE HANDS SPOTLESS.

I'VE SCRUBBED THEM TO THE BONE.

3 Add a dessertspoonful of sweetcorn to the mixture. (Younger readers should ask their adult assistant to open the tin and risk a nasty cut.)

4 Add a dessertspoonful of chocolate cake mix and stir the mix again. Continue stirring until your poo mixture is as dry as you want your poo to be.

5 Pour a little olive oil over the back of your teaspoon and sculpt the mixture into a nice lumpy poo shape.

EVIL IDEA
Dare your little sister that you can eat poo. Eat it and enjoy the horrified look on your family's faces when you offer them a mouthful...

WHAT HAPPENS:

Your homemade poo looks horribly convincing – definitely realistic enough to fool your little sister.

THIS IS BECAUSE:

Poo is a delightful mixture of dead cells, dead germs (plus some live ones) and bits of leftover food your body can't digest. Your homemade poo has far less germs but it does contain sweetcorn husks – a food your body can't digest (that's why they turn up in real poo). The sickening shine of your homemade poo comes from olive oil – in real poo it comes from from fat and mucus from the guts. Enjoy!

OH NO – Dr Grimgrave wants to show us his guide to poo colours! I do apologize for this…

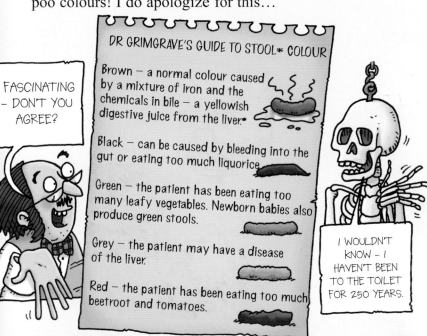

FASCINATING – DON'T YOU AGREE?

DR GRIMGRAVE'S GUIDE TO STOOL* COLOUR

Brown – a normal colour caused by a mixture of iron and the chemicals in bile – a yellowish digestive juice from the liver.

Black – can be caused by bleeding into the gut or eating too much liquorice.

Green – the patient has been eating too many leafy vegetables. Newborn babies also produce green stools.

Grey – the patient may have a disease of the liver.

Red – the patient has been eating too much beetroot and tomatoes.

I WOULDN'T KNOW – I HAVEN'T BEEN TO THE TOILET FOR 250 YEARS.

* MEDICAL TERM FOR A LUMP OF POO.

GREEDY GUTS QUIZ

This queasy quiz is sure to whet your appetite – just so long as you can work out what Dr Grimgrave is talking about!

1. MY IDIOT PATIENTS DO THIS ABOUT 15 TIMES A DAY. THEY EVEN DO IT IN MY SURGERY!

2. IN 1794 DR THOMAS BEDDOES INVENTED A MACHINE THAT MADE HIS PATIENTS DO THIS. IT HAD NO MEDICAL USE WHATSOEVER – GRR! THAT IDIOT DOCTOR WAS A DISGRACE TO THE MEDICAL PROFESSION!

3. THIS TRAVELS THROUGH THE BODY IN 30–45 MINUTES.

4. THIS CONTAINS A WASTE SUBSTANCE ALSO FOUND IN URINE (OR "WEE" AS MY IDIOT PATIENTS CALL IT).

POSSIBLE ANSWERS (with English translations)

a) Saliva (that's "spit" to you)

b) Intestinal eructation (fart)

c) Belch (burp)

d) Regurgitation (sick)

Answers:

1 c) Roughly. Why not try counting them? But don't try adding to your score – especially during posh dinner parties. By the way you can have half a point if you said b) since the figure here is about 10–15 (but don't let them out at posh dinner parties either).

2 d) It was a chair that whizzed round and round and until the patient's breakfast shot from their mouth and splattered anyone standing too close.

3 b) Next time you eat food that makes you windy, why not time how fast the effects appear?

4 d) The substance is called urea. So last time you had a wee did you actually dribbled a little wee – or something like it.

BONES, GROANS AND TREMBLING TEETH

BONES ARE YOUR BODY'S SCAFFOLDING – HOLDING THE REST OF YOU UP SO YOU DON'T FLOP TO THE FLOOR IN A BLUBBERY BLOB. AND THEY'RE LEVERS TO HELP YOUR MUSCLES MOVE YOUR BODY BITS...

(SO THERE'S NO EXCUSE FOR NOT TAKING EXERCISE.)

FEEL THE VIBE

What's this? Dr G is humming – could he be in danger of being happy?

WHAT YOU NEED:
• **Yourself**

WHAT YOU DO:
1 Close your lips. Make sure your upper and lower teeth are touching but your jaws aren't clenched, otherwise you can't do the experiment.

2 Try humming at different levels. Start as low as you can and try a higher note, and so on.

WHAT HAPPENS:

At certain notes you hear and feel a buzz and tingle as your teeth vibrate (wobble fast) and chatter together. In fact, the louder you hum the more your teeth tingle.

THIS IS BECAUSE:

Anything that vibrates makes a sound. The vibes spread through air, water and solid objects in the form of waves called soundwaves… And er, help – any ideas Dr G?

WE MAKE SOUNDS WITH THE VOCAL CORDS IN OUR WINDPIPES. THE VOCAL CORDS VIBRATE AND SET OFF SOUNDWAVES THAT SPREAD THROUGH THE AIR AND YOUR HEAD. THEY EVEN MAKE YOUR TEETH VIBRATE.

Bet you never knew!

Your voice gets its tone from the shape of the air spaces and bones inside your skull. They're unique to you – and that means that no one has a voice quite like yours.

BLAH! BLAH! BLAH!

MAYBE THAT'S WHY HE LIKES THE SOUND OF HIS SO MUCH…

TEST YOUR TENDONS

HERE'S A SIMPLE EXPERIMENT THAT EVEN MY IDIOT PATIENTS CAN ATTEMPT.

AND YOU DON'T NEED A BRAIN TO TRY IT...

WHAT YOU NEED:

- **Your hand complete with all your fingers**
  (you can count them to make sure they're all there)
- **A table** • **A pen or pencil**

WHAT YOU DO:

1 Pretend your hand is a giant sinister spider. Touch the table top with your fingertips.

TWITCH

EEK!

2 Curl your middle finger underneath itself. You may need your other hand for this job. Tuck the pen into the crook of the finger.

3 Now for the tricky bit. Starting with your thumb, try to lift each of your fingertips off the table.

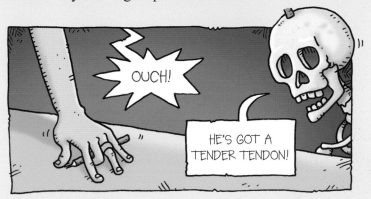

OUCH!

HE'S GOT A TENDER TENDON!

WHAT HAPPENS:
Yikes – you can't lift your ring finger (that's your fourth one). Are you going to be stuck like this for life?

THIS IS BECAUSE:
Probably not – let's check Dr G's casebook...

DR GRIMGRAVE'S CASEBOOK

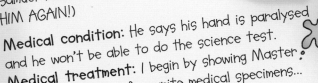

Name of idiot patient:
Samuel Watkins (Sigh – NOT HIM AGAIN!)

Medical condition: He says his hand is paralysed and he won't be able to do the science test.

Medical treatment: I begin by showing Master Watkins one of my favourite medical specimens...

The patient turns green and looks even greener when I suggest that he might like to donate his hand for medical research. Soon afterwards he leaves the surgery at top speed. His hand seems to have made an amazing recovery.

Medical notes: The muscles are attached to the bones by tough cords called tendons. When a muscle pulls, the tendon pulls the bone. As an experienced doctor I know that the third and fourth fingers are attached to the same tendon and when the tendon's pulling on one finger it can't move the other.

WHAT YOU DO:

1 Phone the Public Health people and ask them to evacuate your street.

2 Take your sock off and inspect your toes. Try to wriggle your little toe without moving the others.

3 Hold up your hand (either one will do – or if you're a bit of a show-off you could even try both at once). Hold your fingers together. Can you move your third and fourth fingers apart to make a "V" shape whilst the other fingers stay together?

4 Hold your thumb like this and imagine you're hitching a lift (no need to stand by a busy road). Does the tip of your thumb bend backwards? Oh look – here's Dr G…

5 Put your fingers together and hold up your hand. Can you bend just the top joint of your little fingers without moving the other fingers?

WHAT HAPPENS:

You may be able to do some but not all of these tests…

ON THE OTHER HAND (OR SHOULD I SAY "THE OTHER FOOT"?) YOU MAY BE ABLE TO DO NONE OF THEM … OR ALL OF THEM!

THIS IS BECAUSE:

The ability to move your fingers and toes in these ways is often called "double-jointed"...

GRRR – HOKUM! BALDERDASH, PIFFLE! IT'S NOTHING TO DO WITH JOINTS – IT'S ACTUALLY TO DO WITH THE ARRANGEMENT OF THE TENDONS AND HOW MUCH MOVEMENT THEY ALLOW EACH OF YOUR FINGERS AND TOES...

The arrangement of your tendons, like everything else to do with your body, is controlled by your genes. You inherited your genes from your parents, but even your brothers and sisters don't have the same genes as you. That's why they look different, and why they may not be able to move their fingers and toes in the same way as you. Why not test them?

Bet you never knew!

In 2001 a performer at the Netherlands National Circus found himself in an awkward position. To be exact, his right foot was over his left shoulder. "I just got stuck" said the 21-year-old contortionist. Sadly the audience thought his cries for help were all part of the act...

HELP – I'M STILL STUCK!

GIVE ME STRENGTH!

WHAT YOU NEED:
- Your muscles
- A set of bathroom scales
- Notebook and pencil
- A good friend (not essential)

WHAT YOU DO:

1 In this experiment you are going to use the scales to measure your strength. Try holding the scales like this and pushing with all your strength.

2 Or using your feet like this (you may need your adult assistant to hold the scales to begin with)…

3 Ask your friend to write down the reading shown on the scales. Then they could try the experiment and you could note down their score. What do the scales say about your strength?

YOU'VE GOT NO MUSCLES.

GRRR!

WHAT HAPPENS:

Your muscles make your hands or feet push on the scales with a force equal to the reading shown on the scales.

THIS IS BECAUSE:

You can imagine muscles as being made of lengths of elastic, but instead of stretching, they shorten to pull on your bones. But although muscles can't push only pull – the arrangement of your bones and tendons allow a muscle to pull and still have the effect of pushing your arms or legs.

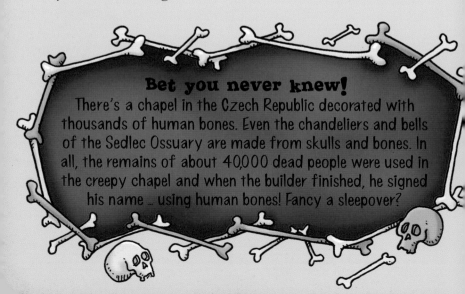

BICEPS PULL TO BEND FOREARM

TRICEPS PULL TO STRAIGHTEN FOREARM

Bet you never knew!

There's a chapel in the Czech Republic decorated with thousands of human bones. Even the chandeliers and bells of the Sedlec Ossuary are made from skulls and bones. In all, the remains of about 40,000 dead people were used in the creepy chapel and when the builder finished, he signed his name ... using human bones! Fancy a sleepover?

RATTLING GOOD
Quiz

OH NO! One of Dr Grimgrave's "idiot' patients has muddled up the bones of his skeleton! Can you spot FIVE mistakes that need to be put right. You can have a "BONE-us" (groan!) point for each bone you can name in your answer…

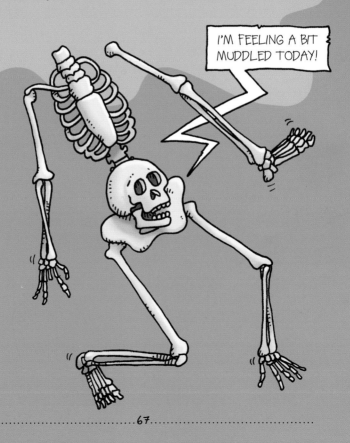

Answers:

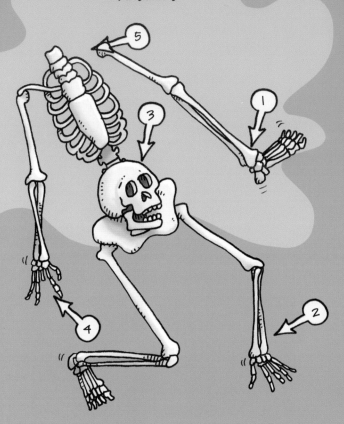

1 The lower left leg (tibia and fibula) and foot bones are where the left forearm should be.

2 The left forearm (radius and ulna) and left hand bones are where the left lower leg should be.

3 The skull is at the bottom of the backbone rather than the top.

4 There is a finger bone – phalange (fa–lan–ge) missing from the right hand.

5 The skeleton's left collarbone (clavicle) is missing.

EYE-POPPING EXPERIMENTS

Can you see this page? Well, hopefully you can – and it's all thanks to your very own pair of state of the art motion sensing, colour imaging, self-cleaning, remote controlled, stereoscopic light detection units. So what am I jabbering on about? Your eyeballs of course!

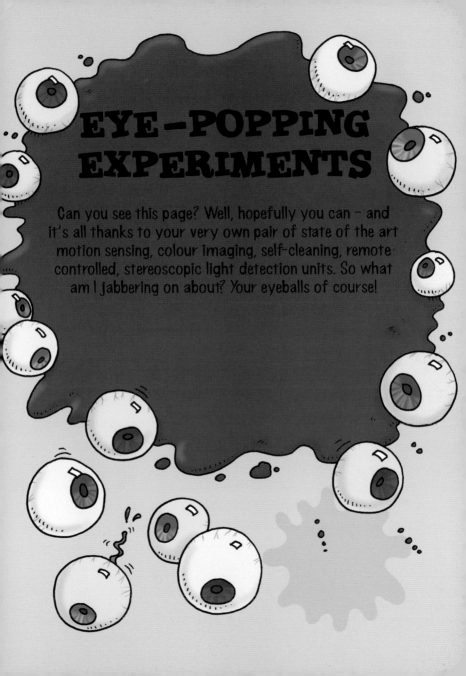

EYEBALL THIS!

Surely Dr G's gone too far this time? You'll just have to try this experiment and find out what he's up to…

WHAT YOU NEED:

- **A nice sunny day**
- **A plastic straw**
- **Nail scissors**
- **Some bubble mixture (if you haven't got any you can mix 200 ml of warm water with a few drops of washing-up liquid. Stir well and don't let your little brother drink it)**

WHAT YOU DO:

1 Cut the end of the straw to look like this. (Younger readers should order their adult assistant to attempt the tricky cutting job and stand by with some bandages and soothing ointment just in case they cut their fingers off.)

2 Close the curtains so that only a slit of sunlight can get into the room from the outside.

3 Dip the cut end of your straw in the bubble mixture.

4 Gently blow a bubble. (Who said science isn't fun? Bubble blowing should be part of every science lesson and not just when your teacher froths at the mouth.) Hold the bubble on the end of the straw so that the light from the window shines on it.

> **TERRIBLE TIP**
> If the bubble gets smaller you can blow gently through the end of the straw to keep it big.

5 Look carefully at the reflection of the scene outside the window on the inside surface of the bubble.

WHAT HAPPENS:

You can see the scene reflected on the outside of the bubble. But the reflection on the inside surface of the bubble is upside down and the wrong way round.

THIS IS BECAUSE:

In order to explain this eerie effect, Dr Grimgrave has invited us to join him at the local hospital, where he has an evening job...

> THERE'S NOTHING I LIKE MORE AFTER A HARD DAY DEALING WITH IDIOT PATIENTS THAN CUTTING UP A BODY IN THE LOCAL MORGUE – AT LEAST THEY DON'T COMPLAIN, HA HA!
>
> THIS EYEBALL IS FASCINATING – JUST TAKE A CLOSER LOOK...

SQUIDGE

LENS

CORNEA

RETINA

PUPIL

DRIP

Normally light is focused by the lens and cornea in the eyeball – but everything your eyeballs see is actually upside down and the wrong way round. Your brain sorts this out before you start trying to walk on the ceiling...

SEEING IS BELIEVING

THIS EXPERIMENT IS FASCINATING. YOU CAN SEE THE END OF YOUR THUMB DISAPPEAR. IT'S A BIT LIKE MY FOUNTAIN PENS – THEY DISAPPEAR WHEN DR SNEAK IS AROUND...

WHAT DR G DOESN'T SEE.)

SWIPE!

WHAT YOU NEED:

- **A thumb (well, what did you expect – an aardvark?)**
- **Two eyes (or three if you happen to be an alien)**

WHAT YOU DO:

1 Turn to face a pale wall. Close your left eye and keep it closed.

2 Hold your right arm out straight with your thumb pointing upwards about 45 cm from your nose.

TERRIBLE TIP
Don't look at your thumb. It helps if there is something interesting on the wall to look at slightly to the left of the thumb.

NOW THAT'S WHAT I CALL INTERESTING!

3 Keep looking at that ever-so interesting object as you s-l-o-w-l-y move your thumb (and the rest of your arm) to the right.

WHAT HAPPENS:

Ooops – the tip of your thumb has disappeared. So have you absent-mindedly popped it in the bacon slicer?

TERRIBLE TIP
If your thumb tip doesn't disappear you might like to re-try the experiment looking through your left eye instead of your right.

THIS IS BECAUSE:

Oh dear – Dr Grimgrave still has that revolting half eyeball from the previous experiment. Hold on to your breakfast – this is going to be beastly... The area where the nerves run from the retina to the brain can't detect light – that's why it's called the "blind spot".Or fovea *as doctors call it. When the end of your thumb is focused on the blind spot, it seems to vanish because your eyeball can't see it.*

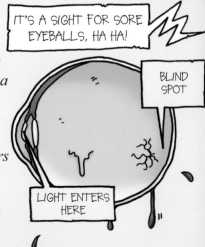

IT'S A SIGHT FOR SORE EYEBALLS, HA HA!

BLIND SPOT

LIGHT ENTERS HERE

NOW YOU SEE IT...

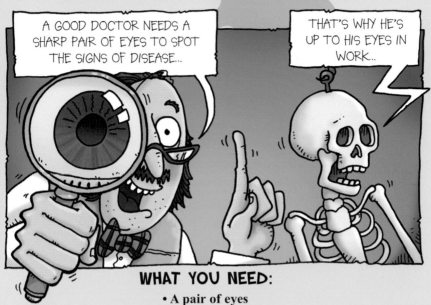

A GOOD DOCTOR NEEDS A SHARP PAIR OF EYES TO SPOT THE SIGNS OF DISEASE...

THAT'S WHY HE'S UP TO HIS EYES IN WORK...

WHAT YOU NEED:

- A pair of eyes
- A good friend or adult assistant
- A table (but don't use Granny's priceless mahogany dining table; if you do you're on your own – OK?)
- Blu-Tack • Protractor • 40 cm of string
- Square of thick cardboard (10 cm x 10 cm)
- Drawing pin • Sheet of flipchart paper or a large old newspaper (but not one with the football results that your dad hasn't read)
- Measuring tape for checking distances • Scissors
- Two sheets of cardboard 15 cm square (or you could use one sheet of double-thickness cardboard) • Two pencils
- Notebook • This book • Photocopier

WHAT YOU DO:

1 Photocopy or trace this disgustingly scary alien monster and colour it in snot green or whatever foul colour you prefer – just so long as it's not black, white or grey. Cut out your completed masterpiece.

2 Spread the large sheet of paper or newspaper on the table and secure it with Blu-Tack.

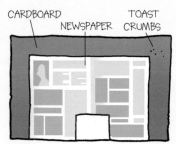

CARDBOARD
NEWSPAPER
TOAST CRUMBS

3 Place the two pieces of cardboard over the paper at the centre of the long side of the table so that your experiment looks like this. Secure the cardboard to the paper with Blu-Tack.

4 Tie the string to the pencil and pin the other end of the string to the centre of the top piece of cardboard. Stick your monster picture to the pencil above the string with Blu-Tack. Use more Blu-Tack to stick the second pencil upright in position X. Your experiment should look like this…

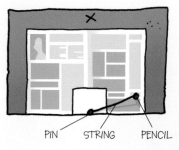

PIN   STRING   PENCIL

YOUR EXPERIMENT SHOULD LOOK LIKE THIS TO A PASSING FLY…

YIKES!

5 Now for the fun bit!

FUN? GRR – THIS IS MEANT TO BE A SERIOUS BOOK OF AN EDUCATIONAL NATURE!

In this *seriously educational* bit you kneel on the floor with your nose level with the table and the drawing pin. You should look steadily at the upright pencil. Ask your assistant to pull the string tight and s-l-o-w-l-y move the pencil with the monster attached in a semi-circle from right to left.

6 When you glimpse the monster out of the corner of your eye, call out "MONSTER!" Your helper should measure the angle of the string from the drawing pin and note down this figure.

MONSTER!!

7 They should continue to move the pencil with the monster on it. When you're sure you can see the colour of the monster, you should call out "MONSTER!" again. Your helper can once again measure this angle.

WHAT HAPPENS:

The first thing you can see through the corner of your eye is the SHAPE of the monster. The colour is harder to make out at this stage – yes, Dr Grimgrave?

THIS IS BECAUSE:

YOUR EYEBALL CONTAINS TWO TYPES OF CELLS – RODS TO DETECT LIGHT AND BASIC SHAPES, AND CONES THAT ARE SENSITIVE TO COLOURS...

THEY'RE NOTHING TO DO WITH FISHING RODS AND ROAD CONES...

Most of your cones are clustered in the centre of your retina at the back of your eyeball. That means that you see colours best when they're in front of your nose. There are more rods around the edges of your retina and that means you can see the shapes of things out of the corner of your eye before you can see the colour.

PERSONALLY I THINK COLOUR IS OVER-RATED I'D PREFER THIS BOOK TO BE IN BLACK AND WHITE...

I'D STILL BE A TASTEFUL SHADE OF GREY.

OUR LOWLY ILLUSTRATOR

DOUBLE TROUBLE

DR SNEAK BANGED HIS HEAD AND NOW HE SEES TWO OF EVERYTHING. I TOLD HIM TO SEE ME AT THE DOUBLE, HA HA!

HE'S ALL HEART – UNLIKE ME. I DON'T HAVE A HEART.

PAT PAT

WHAT YOU NEED:
• Your scary alien monster stuck to the pencil from the previous experiment – and if you haven't tried that experiment yet, you'll have to make it

WHAT YOU DO:
1 Hold the monster at arm's length.

2 Feeling brave? Great – now slowly move the pencil and monster towards your face.

3 Then repeat this step with one eye closed.

WHAT HAPPENS:

OH HORRORS! At a certain distance you see not one but TWO monsters! Are they breeding, Dr Grimgrave?

THIS IS BECAUSE:

GRR – DON'T BE RIDICULOUS! IT'S ALL TO DO WITH STEREOSCOPIC VISION.*

Each eye sees slightly different views of the world because they're slightly apart. Normally your brain puts the two views together to make a single 3-dimensional picture. But as you bring the monster closer, each eye sees the monster against a different background. The only way your brain makes sense of this is to assume there are two monsters. So that's what you see.

THAT ANNOYING FLY FROM PAGE 76.

GRR – UNHYGIENIC FLY!

HMM – I'M IN TWO MINDS ABOUT THIS EXPERIMENT...

AND I'VE GOT NO MIND AT ALL.

*ENGLISH TRANSLATION = YOU'RE ACTUALLY SEEING TWO VIEWS.

APPALLING
EYEBALL Quiz

Here's a beastly little treat for your stereoscopic vision…

Match the eyeball to the animal, but beware – one eyeball will be left
over at the end of the quiz and one of these animals will still be missing
an eyeball…

2 This eyeball is the size
of a table–tennis ball.

1 This eyeball can detect
X–rays.

Animals to consider
a) Cat
b) Ostrich
c) Giant squid
d) Human

3 This eyeball contains
a reflective layer behind
the retina to detect
more light at night.

4 This eyeball is the
size of a basketball.

LICK

SENSELESS EXPERIMENTS

Would you fancy being a potato in a dustbin? Sounds like a rubbish life to me. I mean, you'd have no senses to tell you about the world. So why not get in TOUCH with your inner self and SNIFF out some TASTEFUL experiments and... (OK, that's enough sense jokes for now — the editor).

SNIFF

A TOUCHY SUBJECT

Run for the hills, readers! Dr Grimgrave's in a strop!*

GRR – BLATHERING IDIOT PATIENTS! WHAT DO THEY EXPECT ME TO DO – CURE THEM? GRR – I'M ONLY A DOCTOR!

SLAM!!

HE'S A BIT TOUCHY WHEN A PATIENT GETS ON HIS NERVES...

*SO WHAT'S NEW?

But then I guess we're all a bit touchy-feely thanks to our nerves. The question is, have you got the nerve to try this experiment?

WHAT YOU NEED:

• A good friend (a very good friend as you will see). They should be dressed in a tee-shirt and a pair of trousers with a pocket
• A blindfold (you could use a sleeping mask, a scarf or a clean cloth) • 2 teaspoons • A few coins of different sizes (make sure your friend doesn't see them. You could get the coins from your adult assistant. (With a bit of luck they'll have forgotten that you spent their coins on page 23) • Five objects of different sizes – I used a shell, a small fork, a pencil sharpener, an egg and a banana

WHAT YOU DO:

1 Carefully place the coins in your friend's pocket. Make sure they don't see them.

2 Challenge your friend to tell you what the coins are by touch. (Make sure they give you the coins back – that's why they have to be a very good friend.)

GRR – DR SNEAK POCKETED 50 PENCE!

3 Blindfold your friend. It's important that they don't see your collection of objects. Gently touch three of the objects on the back of your friend's arm one after the other. Turn each object so that they can feel it from all angles and then ask them to tell you what the object is.

4 Now give your friend the two teaspoons. Help them touch the two remaining objects with the rounded side of the spoon. Can they work out what they're touching?

FOR STAGE 3, I USED AN ICE CUBE, MY SHRUNKEN HEAD AND A HUMAN HAND. YOU SHOULD HAVE USED DR SNEAK'S FACE!

LAUGH? I NEARLY CRACKED MY JAWBONE!

WHAT HAPPENS:

Most people easily identify coins using their sense of touch. Step 3 is harder and Step 4 is even more difficult.

THIS IS BECAUSE:

This experiment tests your friend's sense of touch. They could tell you what the coins were more easily than the objects because they have more touch sensors in their fingertips than the backs of their arms. Step 4 is more difficult because they can't feel the objects at all — only work out their shape. You can expect some very strange suggestions...

IS IT BREAD?

HE OUGHT TO USE HIS LOAF!

Bet you never knew!

You have touch sensors for light pressure and stroking. They're the nice ones. Others detect when someone is prodding you and shaking your body. And then there's another sensation brought to your brain from nerve endings in your skin — PAIN!

HA HA! YOU'RE KILLING ME!

TICKLE

TICKLE

TICKLE

WAIT A MOMENT – I'M ALREADY DEAD!

FALLING DOWN

We join Dr Grimgrave in a moment of crisis…

So what's going on? Well, this experiment for a start…

WHAT YOU NEED:
• **Your body** • **Two pillows**

WHAT YOU DO:
1 Take off your shoes.

2 Place the two pillows on the floor – one on top of the other and stand on them. Slowly raise one leg and lift your arms.

3 Repeat step 2 with your eyes closed.

WHAT HAPPENS:

Step 2 is difficult but possible. Step 3 isn't so possible and you may lose your balance.

THIS IS BECAUSE:

It's all to do with a very strange structure in your inner ear that looks like an alien snail. Here's one from Dr Grimgrave's medical collection…

COCHLEA MEANS "SNAIL" – CAN YOU SEE WHY?

ANTI-SOCIAL SNAIL

SEMI-CIRCULAR CANALS

COCHLEA

Your semi-circular canals contain fluid and tiny hairs that detect swilling movements in the liquid. Nerves take the sensation to your brain. Normally your brain has the info from your eyes to double-check data from your inner-ear, and it moves your body to help you keep your balance. But when you shut your eyes this isn't possible and that's why it's easier to fall over…

I'M FALLING DOWN ON THE JOB

HEAR EAR

Dr Grimgrave loves listening to classical music at a deafening volume. But how *sound* is your hearing?

IT'S LOUD ENOUGH TO WAKE THE DEAD!

WHAT YOU NEED:
- A table • A large room
- Tape measure • 30-cm ruler
- Pin or needle • Notebook and pencil
- An elderly volunteer (if you're very brave you could ask an elderly teacher) • Radio or any portable music player

WHAT YOU DO:
1 Make sure it's completely quiet.

2 Get your volunteer to stand with their back to the table and take two paces away from it.

3 Drop the pin on the table from a height of 30 cm. Can they hear the sound?

4 Repeat step 2 until the volunteer can't hear the sound.

Use the tape measure to find the distance to the table and note down this figure.

5 Repeat steps 3 and 4 but this time your volunteer is dropping the pin and you're trying to hear it.

6 Now for the second stage of the experiment. Switch on the radio. Close your eyes and turn on the spot a few times.

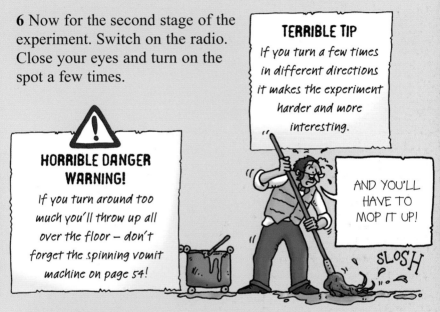

TERRIBLE TIP

If you turn a few times in different directions it makes the experiment harder and more interesting.

HORRIBLE DANGER WARNING!

If you turn around too much you'll throw up all over the floor – don't forget the spinning vomit machine on page 54!

AND YOU'LL HAVE TO MOP IT UP!

SLOSH

7 Stop turning and without opening your eyes try to point in the direction of the radio.

8 Put a finger in one of your ears and repeat steps 5 and 6.

WHAT HAPPENS:

1 You should be able to detect the sound of pin dropping at a greater distance than your elderly volunteer.

2 It's harder to judge the position of the radio with one finger stuck in your ear.

THIS IS BECAUSE:

The elderly volunteer can't hear as well as you because…

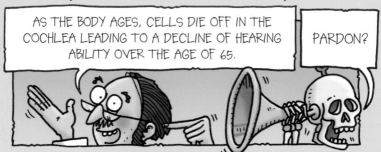

AS THE BODY AGES, CELLS DIE OFF IN THE COCHLEA LEADING TO A DECLINE OF HEARING ABILITY OVER THE AGE OF 65.

PARDON?

The second stage of the experiment shows why you need two ears. Your brain compares the directions of the sound picked up by each ear to judge where the sound is coming from.

WAGGLE

WHEN ONE EAR IS BLOCKED THIS BECOMES MORE DIFFICULT.

Bet you never knew!

Your ears and nose carry on growing for the rest of your life. The increase in size is small but if you lived to be 500 you might look like Dumbo the elephant.

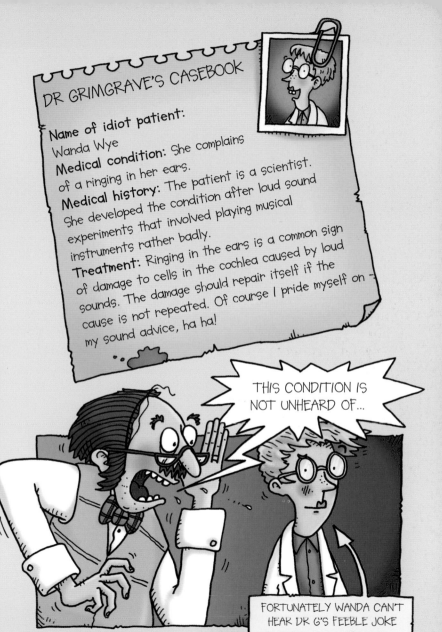

DR GRIMGRAVE'S CASEBOOK

Name of idiot patient:
Wanda Wye

Medical condition: She complains of a ringing in her ears.

Medical history: The patient is a scientist. She developed the condition after loud sound experiments that involved playing musical instruments rather badly.

Treatment: Ringing in the ears is a common sign of damage to cells in the cochlea caused by loud sounds. The damage should repair itself if the cause is not repeated. Of course I pride myself on my sound advice, ha ha!

THIS CONDITION IS NOT UNHEARD OF...

FORTUNATELY WANDA CAN'T HEAR DR G'S FEEBLE JOKE

THE SENSIBLE SENSE Quiz

I bet you've got far too much good sense to come to grief in this tricky test. Well, you have – haven't you?

TRUE or FALSE?

1 You can get used to even the most disgusting smells.

2 In the 1980s food scientists invented tadpole-flavoured crisps.

3 In 2002 Japanese scientists grew an artificial eyeball.

4 The inside of your nose is the only place in your body where your nerves meet the outside air.

Answers:

1 TRUE – this is said to be true. It explains why people are able to work in smelly factories or school kitchens.

2 FALSE – but they did invent hedgehog-flavoured crisps (don't panic – it didn't contain real hedgehogs). Other freaky flavours included strawberry and mince-pie-flavoured crisps. Feeling peckish?

3 TRUE – scientists at Tokyo University removed a tadpole's eyeball and then helped it grow a new one. Well, that's all right then.

4 TRUE – they're the nerves used to detect whiffs in the air. In fact they're usually covered by a thick layer of protective snot – lovely!

EPILOGUE:
THE BEASTLY BODY OF EVIDENCE

Sadly we've come to the end of this beastly book.
Oh don't look so sad! Oh, OK – here's one last
experiment just for you! It's based on something that
happens to us all…

TOOTH TRUTHS

OLD AGE COMES TO US ALL UNFORTUNATELY…

IT CAME TO ME.

HAPPY DEATH-DAY!

WHAT YOU NEED:

- **A tape measure or ruler**
- **Notebook and pencil**
- **Yourself (complete with all your available teeth)**
- **An elderly adult (it helps if they're related to you and they've still got a brain and a few of their own teeth)**

WHAT YOU DO:

1 Inform your volunteer that this is a serious experiment in the interests of scientific research and not an excuse to be cheeky about their age. (Keep a straight face and they might believe you.)

2 Carefully measure the distance between your gums and the end of one of the big front teeth of your upper jaw (body experts call these teeth "incisors"). Note this figure.

3 Repeat step 2 for your elderly volunteer – not a very pleasant task – especially if they haven't brushed their teeth for a 250 years. Once again note the result.

WHAT HAPPENS:

Your elderly volunteer's teeth are far longer than yours.

HMM – FASCINATING...

YOU'RE ABOUT 300 YEARS OLD...

THERE'S NO NEED TO GET PERSONAL.

THIS IS BECAUSE:

As a person ages their gums tend to shrink – exposing more of their teeth. This explains why old folk are often described as "long in the tooth".

In the Capuchin Catacombs in Palermo, Sicily you can inspect hundreds of dried-out dead bodies and skeletons. Some of the grisly remains are more than 200 years old but they're all dressed in their finest clothes – ready and waiting for their relatives to pay them a visit.

PING

I WOULDN'T BE SEEN DEAD IN A PLACE LIKE THAT!

Every body gets old sooner or later but on the whole it doesn't do too badly. It plods along year after year and hopefully doesn't go wrong too often. Of course some people are always going to say that the body is "yucky" or "beastly". But you know better – don't you?

In fact – having read this book, tried the experiments and trained as a Horrible Scientist you may think that your body is definitely on the amazing side of awesome. After all, you used it to read this book and try these experiments. So it must be a good thing!

I WISH I HAD A BODY...

I WISH I HAD A BRAIN...

DON'T MISS THESE HORRIBLE SCIENCE HANDBOOKS!